Thirty Days of Thoughts About Christian Recovery and the Holidays

Rev. Dr. Kevin T. Coughlin Ph.D.

KTC Publishing Phase IIC Coaching, LLC

This book is a work of nonfiction.

Except where noted; names, characters, places, and incidents are the product of the author's imagination or are used fictitiously. Any resemblance to actual events, locales, or persons, living or dead is coincidental.

First Printing

Printed in the United States of America

ISBN 978-0-9977006-1-9 (paperback)

Introduction

Thirty Days of Thoughts About Christian Recovery and the Holidays is a collection of thoughts, memories, and lessons learned over twenty years of recovery with family and friends. Best-selling author Rev. Dr. Kevin T. Coughlin Ph.D. shares his thoughts, heart, and soul as you travel a journey of thirty days of his thoughts, memories, and lessons learned over two decades of recovery with him.

You can expect this thoughtful little book to bring up some feelings and memories from your lifetime. This honest, heartfelt look at life and some of the truths learned by the author are priceless.

Recovery can be a tough time for some people, depending on their life situations. The Holidays are an extremely hard time of year for those in recovery. If nothing else, perhaps this literary pearl will make us all more aware of the human condition that impacts us all at certain times of our lives.

There's nothing like a good book, a warm drink, a comfortable chair in front of a glowing fireplace on a cold winter's night, where that book makes us think, feel, and want to be a better human being.

Thirty Days of Thoughts About Christian Recovery and the Holidays is the author's tenth book. This book is dedicated to the author's writing coach, Samuel Benjamin Pierson who passed in 2010.

PLEASE VISIT www.theaddiction.expert for other books written and published by Rev. Dr. Kevin T. Coughlin Ph.D., there you can join his mailing lists for advanced notice on his next books, trainings, and live events.

Day One

Fear is powerful and can destroy lives; however, faith is more powerful than fear! Today I am going to take faith that everything in my life is going to work out just as it is supposed to happen. Fear has no power in my life today!

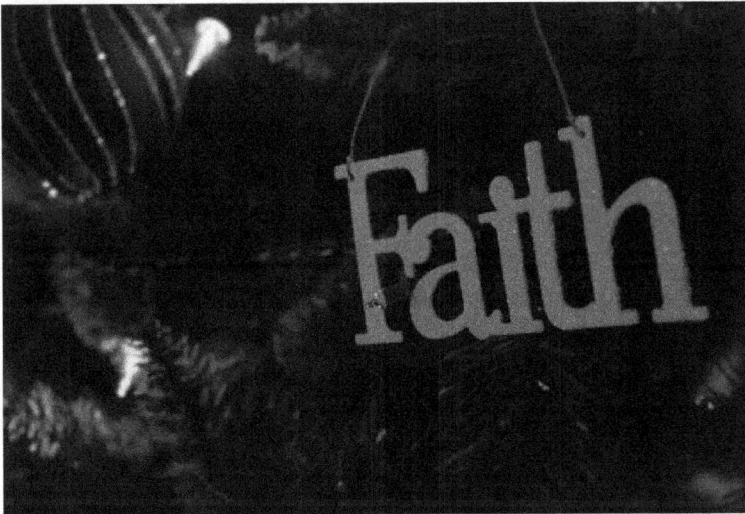

Day Two

God's plan will happen today if I do the footwork that I am responsible for doing to be successful! If God is with me, I cannot fail if I take the necessary action to succeed today.

Day Three

Successful people set goals and follow-up with specific action plans defining who, what, when, why, how, and where, with a partner who holds them accountable on specific timetables. Set goals, plan actions, take actions, follow-up and be very specific for success!

Day Four

I am not alone today. Wherever I am, whatever I am doing, there are other people just like me who have been in the same position who have become very successful and so can I! I am not terminally unique!

Day Five

I cannot isolate today! I need to be around positive, spiritual influences that will encourage success in my life. I need to be in the winner's circle, not the losers cell block! We pick up habits from the people around us. Today, I want to be a success!

Day Six

When I do service work for others, the truth is, that I am really helping myself. Service work builds character, humility, and a great attitude. We are our brother's and sister's keepers.

Day Seven

My attitude today will dictate the quality of my future! I need to be grateful for everything in my life, especially the little things that most people take for granted. I pray that I can stay right sized and keep a good attitude today.

Day Eight

Forgiveness is essential in my life today! I must not harbor resentments, hold grudges, or judge others. My job today is to keep my side of the street clean and help others when I am needed. The price has already been paid at Calvary for all! I am forgiven today!

Day Nine

Today I must walk in truth and honesty. Even the smallest lie, manipulation, or dishonesty will rob me of my spirit-centeredness and balance today. The truth sets us free!

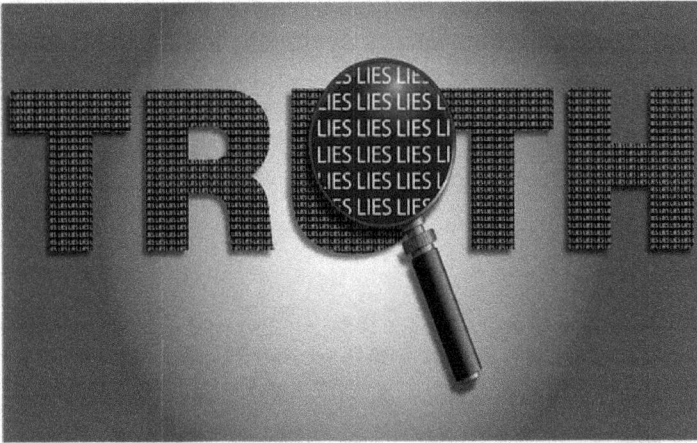

Day Ten

Today I know that I will have much greater success with kindness. I don't have to be a tough guy or try to impress anyone. I don't have to be afraid of other people or shut them out. I can let people into my life today. One of the best ways to get to know others is by sharing my story or history with them. Trust is crucial to relationships. Most of us have been hurt by other people or have hurt other people in life. We must learn to trust again. Today I will take small steps toward trusting others again and letting them into my life.

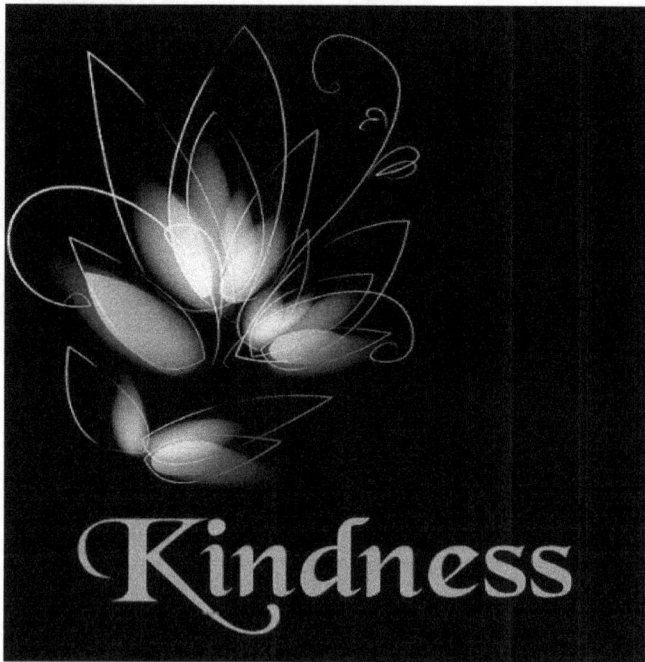

Kindness

Day Eleven

Anger must be managed for success in life today. I can do this by recognizing the signs and symptoms of getting angry such as a raised pulse, turning red, sweating, clenched fists and jaw, increased heart rate. Then I need to remember that anger comes from hurt and fear. I need to ask myself who or what is hurting me, or who or what am I afraid of. Once I identify the source of the anger, I can find a positive way to let go of it, like praying, writing, exercising, walking, sharing with others, etc. If I don't do these things, my anger will be relived and become a resentment and possibly turn into rage. I can't afford resentment and rage in my life today! I must manage any angry feelings and emotions that come up during my day today; it's normal for people to feel and have emotions. It's not normal to have rage and resentments.

Day Twelve

People have no power in my life today unless I let them. What other people think of me is none of my concern as long as I am doing my best to be a good person and keep my side of the street clean and help others. Through life other people will judge us for their own reasons no matter what we do, if we do a thing to please man instead of God, we may be very unhappy and displeased. We cannot serve two Masters. Today I will not give other people power in my life!

Day Thirteen

There are many forms of service work that I can do. There is the great need in the world today. There are homeless shelters, soup kitchens, ministries, food banks, and nursing homes–unlimited opportunities for service work to others. I pray that I will make myself useful to my brothers and sisters today and be of service to God.

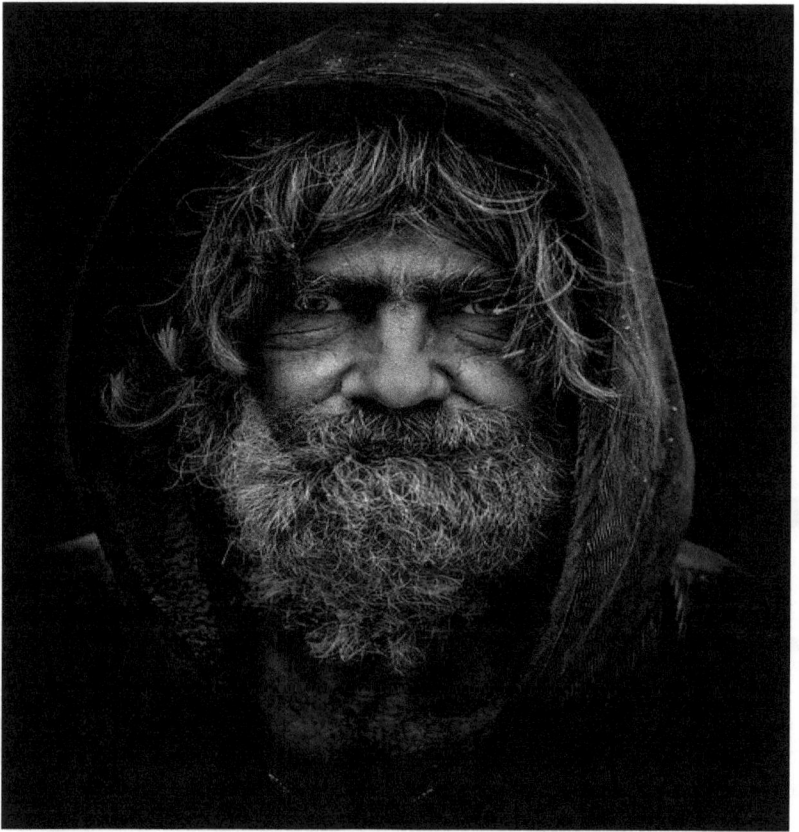

Day Fourteen

Being sober doesn't mean just not using mind and mood altering chemicals. Being sober today means much more; it's about saying yes to life and being a spiritual person, doing the best that I can each day to answer God's call in my life and be of service. Being of sound body, mind, and spirit, and living in the balance, in God's will is what sobriety means to me today.

Day Fifteen

Spirituality today is not about shooting stars and rainbows; it's about saying yes to life and all that is good and right in life. Spirituality is about answering the call in my life and being of service; doing the next right thing as best I can in balance today.

Day Sixteen

True humility today is acknowledging my shortcomings and embracing my gifting; working on my shortcomings and utilizing my gifting to serve God and my brothers and sisters. Humility is not about groveling in the streets.

Day Seventeen

Wisdom comes with time and experience. You can't rush wisdom; it's not something that is supposed to be rushed. It will come in time and with making choices, both good and bad. The experience probably teaches us the most as we take our lumps in life. Like a hand learns to repel from a hot stove, we learn many valuable lessons over the years. Today I will learn life's lessons and not try to rush wisdom.

Day Eighteen

Learning to turn things over to God is one of the greatest lessons that I've learned in life. God will give me what I can handle; however, if it becomes too much, I must turn things over to God's care, so that I may have peace and serenity once again. Life is going to happen on God's terms, no matter what I do. Today I will let go of my problems and let God handle them that I might have peace, joy, and serenity.

Day Nineteen

Some days, all I have to do is just be. I don't have to do anything else but be. We like to make ourselves self-important every day, I need to do this, and I need to do that. However, the truth is, there are days where all I have to do is breathe.

Day Twenty

Prayer and meditation are an important part of my day. These both connect me with God. Meditation is me listening for God's calm still voice, and praying is me talking with God. Meditation also gives me a chance to relax and give my burdens to the Lord.

Day Twenty-One

We all have different gifting. Some individuals are good at many things; others are excellent at one thing; however, we all have some form of gifting. Some people have trouble finding or acknowledging their gifts, but they have them. I have yet to meet a person that is not gifted in some way. I have noticed with age that I have gifts that I never realized before. I give the Lord the credit for all of my gifting; after all, He is my Creator!

Day Twenty-Two

Shame is a killer, just like addiction! I found out early in recovery that I am not alone. That was important to know because I so often felt alone like I was the only person in the world who thought and acted like I did. Once again I found out I am not terminally unique! This helps to get rid of any shame a person might have; remember that shame is an inside job!

SHAME IS A SILENT KILLER!

www.theaddiction.expert

Day Twenty-Three

I must continue to grow spiritually each and every day. I found that I can't stay the same and stay spiritual. They say that you can't live on yesterday's manna or spiritual food. I noticed if I'm not growing spiritually, I'm regressing. I need to make sure that I put myself in life situations where I'm growing spiritually each and every day. Spirituality must be a priority to me today!

Day Twenty-Four

I found out that I am my worst and most harsh critic! I need to be good to myself today. Yes, I need to hold myself accountable; however, I don't need to beat myself up. I need to be good to myself while holding myself accountable today!

Day Twenty-Five

In recovery, I would always hear that meeting makers make it. That is simply not true! This is the truth: meeting makers make it if they work a program of action to change their lives! Meetings without a program leaves out the most important part, the vehicle to change. The program is the vehicle to change, and the fellowship supports that vehicle.

Day Twenty-Six

Sponsors are important in recovery. Their job is to guide people through the steps of recovery. It is not their job to give advice to people on how to live their lives, how long they should stay in treatment, relationships, banking, law, or anything else. Sponsors are guides to the Twelve Steps, period.

Day Twenty-Seven

It's good to have good friends! We all need good people in our lives. It seems like the older we get, the smaller the circle gets. I want to make sure that I treat my close friends right today.

Day Twenty-Eight

The family is important! We only get one family. We can't let anger, resentment, hurts, and other worldly things get in the way of our love for our families. Life goes by faster than we think! It's important to me to honor my family today!

Day Twenty-Nine

I must always honor God! I do this by the way I live my life, the choices that I make each day, the service work that I do, and being my brother's and sister's keeper. I need to honor God's calling in my life today and put Him first above all things.

Day Thirty

We are all students, and we are all teachers! I must continue to learn each day; there is always a new lesson if I am paying attention. God is awesome; check out His word!

Rev. Dr. Kevin T. Coughlin Ph.D. Publication Credits

KTC Publishing Phase IIC Coaching, LLC Amazon.com *30 Days of Thoughts for the Holidays.* 2016 Made the Amazon.com Top 100 Best Seller list.

KTC Publishing Phase IIC Coaching, LLC Amazon.com *Recovery & Life Coaching; The Official Workbook for Coaches and Their Clients.* Co-Author Dr. Cali Estes 2016 #1 Best-Seller Amazon.com Top 100 Best-Seller List

KTC Publishing Phase IIC Coaching, LLC Amazon.com *Addictions: What All Parents Need to Know to Survive the Drug Epidemic.* 2016 Made the Amazon.com Top 100 Best Seller list.

KTC Publishing Phase IIC Coaching, LLC Amazon.com *If You Want What We Have; A Journey Through the Twelve Steps of Recovery Workbook and Manual* 2015 Made the Amazon.com Top 100 Best Seller list.

KTC Publishing Phase IIC Coaching, LLC Amazon.com *In the Sunlight of the Spirit* Workbook and Manual 2015

KTC Publishing Phase IIC Coaching, LLC Amazon.com *We Can; A Collection of Poetry, A Journey Through Addiction and Recovery 2016*

KTC Publishing Phase IIC Coaching, LLC Amazon.com *We Can 2; A Collection of Poetry, A Journey Through Addiction and Recovery 2016*

KTC Publishing Phase IIC Coaching, LLC Amazon.com *We Can 3; A Collection of Poetry, A Journey Through Addiction and Recovery 2016*

Tumbleweeds; Feather Books Poetry Series a Book of Poetry Written by Rev. Kevin T. Coughlin Feather Books England May 2002 (In Memory of DeWitt)

Wayne Independent Newspaper Honesdale, PA

News Eagle, Hawley, PA

Reading Eagle, Reading, PA Berks & Beyond

www.addictsrehab.com

My RecoveryRadio.com Host Kent Paul Sept. 11[Th], 2016 Interview

BBS Radio Poetry reading
Blog Talk Radio - Interviews
The Serenity Show - Interview
Passion Diva Radio- Interview
www.sacredearthpartners.com - Interview
The Broken Brain (Blog Talk Radio) - Interview
www.eatingdisorderhope.com
Keys to Recovery Newspaper Beth Dewey CEO
www.keystorecovery.com
All 4 Ur Addiction Recovery Referral Resource Guide Jenny
Clark Owner
Tripadvisor.com
MindBodyNetwork
Grieving Behind the Badge Peggy Sweeny Founder
www.theaddictsmom.com
In Recovery Magazine
The Sober World Magazine
The Soberworld.com
Shout My Book
Bookgoodies.com
Goodreads
Book Reader Magazine
Awesomegang.com
www.christiancoaches.com
NEWS CHANNEL 10 EYEWITNESS NEWS
CHANNEL.COM
KHQQ6 ABC NEWS
ABC EYEWITNESS NEWS 8 KLKN-TV
FOX14 NEWS AT 9
Erie News Now
NTV Nebraska.TV ABC
Western Mass News Channels 3 ABC 40 Fox 6
ABC9 KTRE
7 KLTV ABC
Fox 19 Now
KXNEWC Eyewitness News
12 WSFA ABC
ABC 6 News WLNE TV
100.7 KFM BFM

Fox 5 KVVU-TV Local Las Vegas
13 WTHR COM Indians News ABC
Eyewitness News 3 WFSB.COM
Fox 12 Oregon
WDRB.COM
Fox29 WFFX.COM
WETV San Diego
HAWAII News Now
Marketers Media
WALB News 10 ABC
Tristate Update.com 13 News WOWK
AM760
WMBF ABC News
KCEN HD ABC KCENTV.COM
WECT6 ABC News
Eyewitness News3 WFSB.COM
WLOX ABC BOUNCE Eyewitness News
Eyewitness News 8
CBS8.COM
News channel 6 KAUZ
SPROUT News
12 Eyewitness News KFVS
KEYC MANKATO News 12 CBS & FOX LOCAL NEWS
3 WRCB TV ABC COM
KNDO 23 NBC
KNDU 25 NBC
The Aurorean, Encircle Publications 1998 Poetry and Essays
Joel's House Publications 1998-2005 Poetry and Essays
Our Journey 1998-2005 Poetry
The Poetry Explosion, The Pen 1999-2003 Poetry
Apostrophe 1998 Poetry
Nuthouse Twin Rivers Press 1998 Poetry
The National Library of Poetry 1998
Lines N' Rhymes 1998 Poetry
The Poetry Church Feather Books
England. Anthology John Hunt Publications 1999 Poetry
A Tapestry in Time. 1999 Poetry Book 18 Poems
Connecticut Department of Mental Health and Addiction Services

The Webster Times 1999 Poetry

The Angel News 1999 Poetry

The Skater won The Editor's Choice Award September 1999 (Our Journey)

The Blind Man's Rainbow 1999 Poetry

Arnazella 2001 Poetry

Feather Books, The Poetry Church 1998-2002

The American Dissident 2002 Poetry

The Good Shepherd Poetry 2002

Ya ' Sou Magazine Essays and Poetry

Colt. Winner Editor's Choice Award Contest Literally Horses 2002

Goodbye My Friend Read on the Radio Rhyme and Reason UBC Europe & the UK September 2001 Read on the Radio in Europe and the UK as a Tribute to those lost on September 11th bombings. My poem was read over the radio for many days.

Tumbleweed Read on BBC Radio in England 2001

Published by Feather Books

Notified by John Waddington Feather that Tumbleweed had been read on BBC Radio in England on Several Occasions.

Stanwich Congregational Flyer Poetry

University of Scranton Panuska College of Professionals Essay 2002

Scranton University 2002 Poetry

The River Reporter Newspaper 2002 Poetry

Unity Community News 2002 Poetry

The Poetry Corner Angelfire.com Poetry

The Poet's Market 2002 Poetry

The Poetry Church England 2003 Poetry

Cover of Wayne Independent News 2003 Poetry

Nomad's Choir 2003 Poetry

Written a series of 9 course manuals for a coaching recovery curriculum. 2014-2015

www.addictedminds.org 2015-2016 Articles Matthew Steiner

www.soberservices.com 2015 Articles

http://fromaddict2advocate.blogspot 2016 Articles Marilyn Davis

LinkedIn 2014-2016 Articles

Two Drops of Ink S.W. Biddulph 2015- 2016 Poetry/ Articles

The Addict's Mom 2016 Articles Blog
Ghostwriter Articles/ Content2014-2016
KEITV12: The Kingdom Hour- Interview
BlogTalkRadio The Kingdom Hour- Interview

About The Author

Rev. Dr., Kevin T. Coughlin Ph.D., DCC, DDV, DD, IMAC, NCIP is an International Master Coach, trainer, #1 best-selling author, writer, poet, speaker, a Diplomate Christian counselor, and therapist, he is Board Certified in Family, Developmental, Alcoholism, Substance Abuse, and Grief Counseling, the Reverend is a NCIP interventionist, a Domestic Violence Advocate, Associate Professor for DCU, a Provincial Superintendent (to be consecrated a Bishop in 2016) and so much more; he is an expert in the field of Addiction and Recovery.

He was a Founder and Board Member of a Residential Recovery Facility New Beginning Ministry, Inc. and is President and CEO of Phase IIC Coaching, LLC., The Program Director for The Addictions Academy, and the former Editor in Chief for Addicted Minds & Associates. The Reverend has over forty-seven years of experience with the AA program.

He has been working in the addiction recovery field for almost two decades, has helped thousands of individuals and their families overcome all types of addictions, substance abuse, alcoholism, process addiction, shame and guilt, relationship and communication problems, anger management, inner healing, self-image, interventions and much more. He is a published author and has published thousands of poems and articles published throughout the United States and other Nations, he has been interviewed on numerous radio talk shows, television, published in magazines, newspapers, books, and online publications; he has been featured on ABC, CBS, FOX, NBC, and the BBC in the UK. Rev. Kev is a former State, National & World-Champion Powerlifter, and still holds several records. He loves to write, read, teach, listen to music, and spend time with people and dogs. His parents are his heroes.

Rev. Dr. Kev's Social Media Accounts

https://www.goodreads.com/author/show/14874631.Kevin_Coug hln

About Me Links:

https://about.me/ktc1961/

http://ilikeebooks.com/if-you-want-what-we-have/

http://awesomegang.com

www.amazon.com/Rev.-Kevin-TCoughlin/e/B01AF6AAAI/ref=ntt_dp_epwbk_0

http://www.barnesandnoble.com/w/addictions-what-all-parents-need-to-know-to-survive-the-drug-epidemic-rev-dr-kevin-t-coughlin-phd/1124049106?ean=9780997700695

http://www.barnesandnoble.com/w/in-the-sunlight-of-the-spirit-rev-dr-kevin-t-coughlin/1124049139?ean=9780997700671

http://www.barnesandnoble.com/w/if-you-want-what-we-have-rev-dr-kevin-t-coughlin/1124049130?ean=9780997700688

http://mybookplace.net/in-the-sunlight-of-the-spirit-a

Facebook
1. Kevin Coughlin: https://www.facebook.com/profile.php?id=100008449955607

2. My Group, Resources for those suffering from addiction and their families: https://www.facebook.com/groups/resourcesforthosesufferingfromaddiction/
3. RevKev The Addiction Expert: https://www.facebook.com/RevKev/?fref=ts

LinkedIn
1. Rev. Dr. Kevin T. Coughlin PhD
   https://www.linkedin.com/in/revkevnetwork

Google+
1. Kevin Coughlin
   https://plus.google.com/112400908736308001821/posts
   My Group: The Recovery Community Family and Friends:
   https://plus.google.com/communities/113521225141112811207

Pinterest
1. Kevin Coughlin: https://www.pinterest.com/ktc1961/
2. My Group Board: Recovery We Can
   https://www.pinterest.com/ktc1961/recovery-we-can/

Tumblr
1. https://www.tumblr.com/blog/revkevsrecoveryworld

Instagram
theaddiction.expert

My Websites:
1. www.revkevsrecoveryworld.com
2. theaddiction.expert
3. theaddiction.guru

Rev. Kev's Goodreads Link:
-spirituality-training-manual-and-workbook-by-kevin-coughlin

Thank you for reading my work! If you enjoyed my book, would you consider reviewing it on Amazon.com? We would appreciate your help in getting the word out on how helpful this book can be in someone's life. Thank you so much and God bless you! Phil 4:13

www.ingramcontent.com/pod-product-compliance
Lightning Source LLC
Chambersburg PA
CBHW071750020426
42331CB00008B/2258